Caius Krohnfeldt was born in 2004 in Denver, Colorado. In this somewhat small town, he grew up with an interest in the quiet side of life. He grew up reading with his family and writing poetry. His love for writing has never stopped, and he now pursues a degree in English at the University of Colorado Denver. Wild & Wise is his first publication.

Wild & Wise

Caius Alexander-Acker Krohnfeldt

Wild & Wise

Vanguard Press

VANGUARD PAPERBACK

© Copyright 2024
Caius Alexander-Acker Krohnfeldt

A CIP catalogue record for this title is
available from the British Library.

ISBN 978 1 80016 83794 038 7

*Vanguard Press is an imprint of
Pegasus Elliot Mackenzie Publishers Ltd.*
www.pegasuspublishers.com

First Published in 2024

**Vanguard Press
Sheraton House Castle Park
Cambridge England**

Printed & Bound in Great Britain

To my mom, who raised me with stars in my eyes

I am deeply honored to be able to thank the following people: My grandfather, Les Krohnfeldt, my grandmother, Cindy Krohnfeldt, my father, Mark Krohnfeldt, and my step-mother, Jennifer Krohnfeldt, for treating me like an adult when I came to them with the idea of publishing a book, and making it a financial reality for me as I started college. My brother, Caxton, and my sister, Cara, who read and understood my poetry before anyone else, and who helped me grow up with poetry and stories. My step-brother, Carter Novinger, who was always willing to read my bits of scratch paper before they became anything at all, the only reason I still write anything at all. Addison Page who took time out of studying for finals to read and edit my poetry and stories, and who contributed more to the writing of these poems than anyone else. All my friends throughout high school who did not bully me for writing poetry. My English teachers, Angela Dryer and Eliot Wilson, who prompted me to write some of my best and who were never afraid to be honest and critical of my work, even outside their classes. The entire team at Pegasus Publishing who made this dream a reality and have been nothing but helpful and kind.

Contents

THE FLIGHT, THE FALL

I remember now, only joy. Only my smile. Only my laughter. Only the warmth and safety of the rushing air as I fell. There was no fear, nor sorrow, nor anger. Just the joy, the flight and the fall. And now I've seen it all. All there ever was to see. All life. All death. All that was ever good or bad in this universe. I have felt the gentle tides of the cosmos wash over me for an eternity, bathing me in warmth and peace and solitude. I have touched time and gently ran my fingers through it. I have let myself be filled with the universe. All that ever was or will be. And now it ends. I approach my final death. And I think back now to the fall. And I leap now once again. This time into entropy. And I am filled once again with joy and peace. And now for the final time, I fall.

I remember being happy as a child. The world was kind to me. Always gentle and serene. Time was not the same then. I'd float through it calmly, unaware of the danger it presented.

That's not to say there were no flaws. But they existed only in the background. Never a fixture of my attention. Maybe that's how things got so out of control with my older brother. Maybe that's why I didn't notice my family breaking to bits.

The day he died was brought to me with nothing but warmth. A soft and quiet breeze, full of sunshine, woke me gently from a lovely dream. A dream where I was kissed by angels gliding down from heavens far above.

At first, there was nothing discernable about this day from all the rest I had lived. Those days, my life had fallen into simple, soothing repetition. Most days were not discernible from any other.

I'd stare out my window every morning, watching the last few minutes of the sunrise. The sunrise that seemed more and more like the same one, every single day. Much like any other day, I would walk throughout my house, mindlessly and aimlessly. After my senior year of school ended, I had a hard time focusing. I could not bring devotion to any one task. So, I would wander, and I'd wonder about what the day would hold.

I found my way into the kitchen, looking for that old, pale-blue kettle. I filled it and placed it on the stove to boil. I didn't mind living alone. I liked the quiet of those mornings. I sat as the water boiled, letting the quiet wash over me with the bright sunlight. I watched as the light hit the dust, dancing like stars in the sun.

I found my way to the bathroom and began to wash my face with cool water. I looked down at my scarred hands in contemplation. I barely recognized them. I found the same unrecognition when my eyes drifted up to that face in the mirror. I stared into my eyes. Sunken slightly from the stress, and I wondered when all that red started to form around the crystal blue that I always thought was my best feature. I gently ran my finger over my slender jawline, feeling for any shaving nicks from the day before.

The longer I gazed the more unrecognizable I became. So, I focused a bit more and tried to comprehend what I was looking at.

Then through that simple quiet came the whistle of the kettle and the shrill ring of the telephone, almost in complete unison, harmonizing with their high-pitched wails.

I moved the kettle quickly off the stove and picked up the phone. I never wanted to answer it, but the noise was worse than any sort of conversation I could have. Or so I thought, at the very least.

"Hello?" I said, with intrigue and a hint of slight annoyance.

"May I speak with Deacon Edwards, please?" the voice replied.

"Speaking. How can I help you?"

"Well, I'm afraid I must be the bearer of bad news this morning," he said, still emotionless.

I gave the response of silence. That comforting silence that kept me safe. If I didn't respond, I would never know.

"Yeah, well, um, I regret to inform you that your brother passed away this morning."

I hung up the phone. I didn't want to know any more. I found out later it was a heroin overdose, but the manner of his death was not my concern. Not right now, anyway. The only thing on my mind was the matter of my own death. And how I could accelerate it.

I walked slowly but with exceptional determination. I did not cry. I did not shake with fear or sorrow. I just walked out to the streets below, surrounded by those immense buildings. Spires of concrete and steel and starlight in the night. And I could hear them whisper. Whisper with the wind that blows between them. Inviting me to climb. And so I did. I climbed.

The parking garage played my footsteps back to me as I walked. It was quiet. Cold, but only in the shadows. One could feel a comforting warmth in the patches of sunlight that jutted through the gaps between the floors. I found myself stopping to run my hands through the sunlight, like one would run their hands through water, dipping my hand in and out of the warmth. And I found myself wondering if there would be starlight in the next life. Or if there would be a next life at all.

The white concrete on the roof managed to blind me quite completely, but only for a moment. I adjusted to the light and breathed in that warm, sunlit air. I walked a little more slowly, savoring my final steps. When I reached the edge, I could not bear to look down at the ground below. I knew that it was far enough. So I looked up to the sky — that great and gorgeous sky. Remembering the kiss of angels. I stepped up to the ledge as if to meet them just a little closer. I breathed just a little heavier now. The air felt thin and unimportant, like something that I didn't want but that was forced into and out of me.

I clenched my fists and grit my teeth and let just one tear fall. I punched my chest with my right hand to force that thin air out, and then… silently and all alone, I took a final breath… and took one step towards nothing.

But then to my immense surprise, I did not fall. I slipped off the ledge, pushed by my own weight. And I floated, spinning slowly towards the center of the street. I saw the ground not moving closer but still far below me. Then far above me. Then as I came around again, far below me once again.

I stopped spinning as I got to the middle of the road. And then, unmoving, I floated there, gasping for breath and staring in shock at my surroundings. I felt suspended, as if in deep water. I floated for only a moment more, breathing deeply in the thick, suspending air. Then I swam; swam through the sunlight above the city. The wind provided me with the only sound up there. I had never felt such ecstasy in all my life. And I never would again. I laughed as I flew, screaming into the wind as I softly rushed through the air. I would climb up till I could feel the oxygen being stripped from my lungs, and then I'd dive back towards the earth, only to gently catch myself above the buildings and the busy streets. This was joy. Joy like I had never felt. Joy that stripped sorrow from my heart and mind. It was freedom and love and warmth. I held happiness in my heart for the last time that day. And as I finally came down from my great flight, the now cold, dark concrete of that parking garage sucked it all out from me. The weight of life returned to me and, in that instant, I could not hear or speak or think. I could not breathe, and the only thing I felt was the gravity pulling tears from my eyes like splinters from sore skin. I was back... and I didn't want to be.

Her face reminded me of the angels from that dream I had so long ago. A kind face. The type that wore a smile nicely. The dimples always made it seem a bit more genuine when she smiled at you. She smiled like she meant it, and that could always make me smile too. She had freckles. Oh, such lovely freckles that draped over the bridge of her nose and onto her soft, high cheekbones. Her hair was always wavy and stopped just above her shoulders. It was dark but had hints of lightness coursing through it, like bits of glowing ember in the remains of a once warm fire. But it was not her smile or her freckles or her hair that reminded me of that angel. It was not the elegance of her walk or the gentleness of her touch. It was her eyes; her bright, blue eyes that held in them the heavens. They were the eyes that looked at me when I stood on that cold rooftop. They were the eyes of that angel who caught me when I almost fell.

Her name was Alexis Deering, and thinking back on her now, she is really one of the only people I have ever truly loved. I met her a few years after my brother passed, just a bit after I began my isolation.

After he died, I grew a great disdain for society. I could not relate to people. I could not understand them. I felt cold and alone. All my thoughts revolved around that day I flew. I wanted to feel that again. I wanted to be happy. But nothing quite compared. Nothing brought me that same happiness.

I dropped out of school just a year before I was supposed to graduate. I took a job for a while, doing some simple data processing. It was low stress and required minimal social interaction. Something I needed with my new state of mind. I saved a great deal of money and moved to the welcoming arms of the Rocky Mountains. I took up residence alone in a small house, thirty minutes away from any sort of civilization in any direction.

My life became routine — too routine for my liking. A gently painful rhythm, that repeated as consistently as the sunset. I made very little money, but I also spent very little. Most of my expenses came from my weekly trip to Celine's, a diner in the small town closest to me.

This is where I would meet her, sitting in that red, synthetic leather booth that tore at all the seams. As with most people, I was not especially warm for quite a while. Never rude or cruel but never too welcoming. This went on for quite some time, close to or just over a year. Every Sunday morning I'd walk in and take a quiet seat at that same booth.

She'd always greet me with a warm, "Hey, stranger," and she'd ask me about my week.

My answer never changed. "Oh, you know, same ol', same ol'," I'd say, over and over.

Nothing changed for quite a while still, but one day she left my check with a bit more of a smile than usual. Something about it seemed more genuine; less forced for more money. And on the check, in small, light lettering, a note…

'My name's Alexis. What's yours?'

For the first time in a while, I let myself smile a bit, and after a bit of contemplation, I wrote back…

'Deacon. It's a pleasure to meet you.'

She greeted me the following day, not with her usual 'Hey, stranger', but instead with a kind of effervescent, 'Morning, Deacon'. God, I'd never seen such brightness as the brightness of her smiling face.

I couldn't help but smile back and say, "Morning Alexis."

Even her wave was gentle as she turned and moved back into the restaurant.

She would go on to ask me out, with another note on my bill, and I responded, of course, with 'yes'. Alexis was the only person in my life that ever made me really smile. She's the only person that ever got me close to being happy. Maybe if I would have gone through with it, then she could have saved me eventually.

I moved in with her, in a small apartment in that same small town. We never fought. I can't remember a single argument. That's not to say it was all good, however. The relationship was more one-sided than I think either of us intended. I loved her, I did, but it was not the same as it was for her. She loved me unconditionally and unequivocally. Nothing to her was more important. I was all there was for her. And while I loved her unconditionally, I could not love her unequivocally. The joy I felt so many years before had broken me. Nothing short of that felt like joy any more. But she could never know. To tell her that her efforts to make me happy were in vain was something I could not bring myself to do. And so I loved her. I loved her all I could. And after five or so more years, when she could no longer wait and finally proposed, I said yes. I said yes, and we set a date — a winter wedding, so often underrated. We would begin the rest of our lives surrounded by warm lights and the gentle falling of cold snow like stars from the sky.

I wanted to be with her. I wanted to make her happy and be able to be happy with her. That's truly all I wanted. And so that December, only a few weeks out from our wedding, I took my fiancé back to the city for a weekend with all the Christmas lights and some long-needed social interaction... Or at least that's what I told her.

The second night we were there, I took myself out of bed early in the morning and got dressed as quietly as I could. I put on my warm peacoat and left our hotel room. On the nightstand, I left a note that read...

'You're all I want, angel. I love you. I'll be back soon.'

I walked back to that rooftop with a smile on my face, my hands deep in my pockets and my nose red from the cold. I was hopeful. Ready to be able to live the rest of my life in complete serenity and happiness. I walked quickly, excited for what was to come, and when I got to the parking garage, I began to run up the stairs, nearly blinded by the brand-new morning sunlight burning through the gaps between the floors. I got to the roof and caught my breath. My heavy breaths shone in the cold morning sunlight.

I took the last few steps towards the edge and once again stepped up to it. And now when I closed my eyes, I saw only her. My angel, Alexis. I smiled, and I cried tears of pure joy. Pure joy at just the thought of her and the thought of finally being happy. I laughed as the tears fell; laughed with excitement and with my arms spread wide towards the sun. And then, I stepped off the roof.

PEPPERMINT

You always smelled like peppermint,
that oil, gum and tea.
And now that scent of peppermint
can always soothe me.

You always smelled like peppermint
In memories just as sweet;
and still as fresh as
peppermint in soft breath.

Whispering jokes into my ear,
Peppermint on the scar
on the back of your neck.
Clinging to your hair
In hugs so close,
I scarcely even remember
being a part of them at all.

It's just you, you
and peppermint.
And now I have to try
To try to not cry,
When sweet, sweet peppermint
passes by.

SUNSHINE HANDS

I told you, I was scared
but it was just a dream.
I told you I was scared
and asked you for a hug.
So you put down your coffee,
the warmth still on your hands.
And I told you I was scared,
that it wasn't just a dream.
So with those sunshine hands of yours,
you wiped away my tears
and told me that you'd be around,
for many good long years.

STARS IN THE SNOW

I see you here beside me
sitting just like me,
with boots up to your knees,
and a coat down to the same
Staring at this snow
and these mountains you loved so.

I see you here beside me,
You try to fix my hair.
You always liked its color,
all fiery and rare.

But truly here beside me
are just shadows on the snow,
Sparkling like the night sky;
Just stars in the snow.

ASTRONOMY

What once was sunshine
Is now just stars;
Cold and dead and far away.
But still they shine;
Even dead
Even gone
Shining in obsidian nights.
Suns are suns,
Even far away;
Cold
and dead
and gone.

ITS GOING TO END SOON

Would you dance with me just once?
Slow and proper just the two of us
Not some silly school dance.
The music's in the corner
Quiet so you have to listen.
Just a dance with you and me
Hands on hips, and hands on shoulders.
Swaying
cheek to cheek.

Old souls and young, all at once
Just dancing
Just moving
but moving together.
Just you and me
some lonely night,
Spinning slowly in the glowing light.
Swaying softly so resigned
Dancing in the end of times.

FROSTY DROPS OF DEW

The grass is hung
with drops of dew.
They froze in the night
They froze along with you.

My mother is frantic
in a dizzy haze,
and rushing about
With the first responders,
Looking for paperwork
to see about resuscitation.

I am staring at the sunlight
Shining through the drops of dew;
Bright and bubbly and scattered
across the yard.
Such precious emerald treasure
those frosty drops of dew.

And then a cloud covers the sun,
and it's just grass now;
And its frozen
All but dead
And so are you.

ETERNITIES ONE HELL OF A GOOD PLACE TO TELL A STORY

So one day I'll be dead
and maybe there's nothing.
Maybe I just die
But there's a chance
that there is some great eternity;
Burning or glowing or
black or who even knows?
But if I go somewhere,
I'll be with you.
And so I have this stupid list
A long and convoluted list,
of all the things you missed.
You missed that movie you said we'd see
You missed my brother Carter,
You missed my freshman year of high school
My first big game and my first dance.
You missed my second sweetheart, my third, fourth, fifth,
and sixth, as well.
You never saw my first real drive. You never saw my car.
You never heard my favorite song or the ones I thought
you'd like.
You never knew I got a job
You missed coming in to visit
I never bought you dinner, or lunch or even breakfast
You missed me getting glasses.

You missed my first plane ride
You missed me pick a college
You missed me make my friends.
You never met my buddy Brody, or his little brother Tate.
You missed all my favorite classes
You never met my favorite teacher
You missed my favorite color change
You don't know how I dress.
You missed the day we moved away and all the days I almost gave up.
You missed my great adventures, the big ones and the small.
If I hadn't known you for a while
at this point I think I'd consider
you a stranger,
knowing nothing more than some passerby
recognizing my face on the street.
But if there is eternity
Some better life after this,
I'll tell you all my stories
about how it all changed.
Like a blissful dressed up child
telling his mother
about the first day of school.

MY GHOSTS SAY HELLO

It's when I'm all alone,
that my ghosts say hello.
The people that left me
Their ghosts that stick around.
My ghosts that only say hello,
when I'm about to drown.

It's when I'm all alone,
that my mother says hello.
My sweet, young mom,
in pain and scared
And wanting an escape.
My sweet, young mom,
who spent too much time
alone at night in her mind.

And it's when I'm all alone,
that Howard says hello.
Silly old Howie,
Who fell in love with the sun as a child,
The sun whose kisses killed him.
Silly old Howie,
who took me on adventures
the last friend he'd ever have.

And it's when I'm all alone,

that she says hello.
The one who got away,
who hasn't talked to me in years.
I've tried but it just doesn't work
The one who got away
who only smiles in my memories
and never walks away.

It's when I'm all alone,
that these ghosts say hello.
The angels that left me,
The ghosts that stick around.

OLD PALS

I stare at water
filling up the sink.
I stare at intersections
of small roads meeting big ones.
I stare at the concrete patterns
from the rooftops of buildings
that seem too short
for it to be worth a shot.
I stare at razors
on Christmas
that children use to open boxes.
I think about my death
Every fucking day.

I used to cower
in corners. Up too late
to even justify sleeping
before school in the morning.
On the verge of tears in fear,
like a toddler
being taught what nightmare means.

But you can read about it
in psych journals and textbooks,
The idea of exposure therapy
Hands in boxes of large spiders.

Thick glass paneling
hundreds of feet in the air.
Behind it all is one very simple idea;
If you face your fear enough
it will probably just go away.

So now I stare
and sit and think
and drift off cliffs
and curbs in my thoughts.

And just wait
just wait for the day,
For death;
that dear old friend of mine
to stop by and say hey.

PURGATORY

I thought it would be cold
but it's not.
I feel the sunshine
through the earth around me.
When it rains
I feel it sinking through me,
Sunlight skies and heaven
coursing under my skin.
I sink a little deeper
and I am wrapped
in roots and stems,
The seeds of flowers
burst in what's left of veins
and bones and organs
and spring forth
Lilies and orchids
that drink the water under my skin.
Someday all these bits and pieces
will shoot away
and become stars.
(and more than likely not
just some gas in space)
But for now it doesn't matter
I just lie here
and somehow some part of me smiles,
Now that I'm just the
flowers and water and sun.

SOME STAR... SOMEWHERE

Some star somewhere
at some indescribable time
is me.
I think about that star
and how it fell in love,
Burning a little brighter
Sunspots blushing
Dancing with some distant star
trying to pull it in.
Closer every lifetime
Hotter day by day.
And soon enough it's melting;
They're melting.
A stellar kiss
that kills planets,
ends lifetimes
just to exist.
A love that means something,
That matters in the end.
They lived for an eternity
to love just only one;
and yes they died
but they died together.
That star and its lover;
God I can't wait
to be a star.

ON THE WANT OF LOVE

To live a life in want of love is to live a life that's never full. It is to live an incomplete, hollow life without any hope for happiness or joy. To live a life in want of love is to be alone and miserable in this world, without anyone to notice your tears or your immense and silent, crushing pain. It is to be desperate for attention and fragile in your ego. It is to live with regret on your shoulders. It is to live a life wondering if it was something you did, or if you are simply that awful. It is to live a life becoming the lonely cynic that people say you are. It is to live a life always wanting more, because the love you have is not the perfect movie love you wished you had, but instead the unrequited love you never wanted.

To live a life in want of love is to settle for love you think you deserve, before quickly realizing that that is not love. It is to want the love of anyone who you pass by, because maybe they love better than the ones who claim to love you now. It is to spend away all that you have earned on gifts and flowers, destined to be thrown away in two weeks' time, if you're lucky enough. It is to be a man who cannot complain about his want of love, for fear of no longer being a man. It is to be a hollow, empty shell in the eyes of all your peers, when you are a woman who cannot love so quickly, and it is to be 'easy' when you love too fast.

To live a life in want of love is to run out of tears before you reach the age of seventeen. It is to cry about being lonely and lost, days before you cry about the blindness and futileness of the love you tried so hard for.

To live a life in want of love is to live with a shattered heart, trembling inside your chest instead of beating. It is to live for true and untainted love but feel lost in the lust of those more broken. It is to want a wife and a husband, but to end up with some shallow partner who soon forgets your name. But to live a life in want of love is not just sorrow and misery — it is hatred and fear, as well. It is to reach for love and hate how short your reach is. It is to love someone completely and hate them for not loving you back. It is to hate your child for reminding you of the love you lost, and it is to hate your parents for misleading you to think that love is real. It is to think of nothing but love and then shy away when it is shown to you, for fear of being hurt more than you already are.

To live a life in want of love is to lose the people you love most preemptively, because you would rather not lose them later when it hurts more. To live a life in want of love is to push those away you love, because you know, deep down, they might not love you back. To live a life in want of love is to never know who really loves you. It is to die alone and have only the ones who truly loved you attend your funeral, after it no longer matters.

THE EXPONENTIAL DECAY OF TIME AND ITS EFFECT ON THE MENTALLY ILL

When I was very young
I made a great decision
that I would take it all
as slowly as I could.
Every breath I took
I would remember
what it means to breathe.

But at some point
in between funerals
and break-ups over
Starbucks tea,
I realized that I had fallen,
Fallen from something high.

It's hard to remember what breathing
means when you're falling.
It's hard to be slow;
It's hard to see
and hard to think
and it's so fast.
I've been falling
for years that blink

by like the drops of rain
you try to track
in the car.

I just need to breathe
but I can't fall forever,
and the faster I fall
the sooner I stop falling.
Just breathe
It'll slow down
Just breathe.
You
won't
even
know
you
stopped
falling.

THE ADDICTIVE PROPERTIES OF
PAIN

Sadness very simply
cannot be boring.
Boring sadness,
the sadness that sits with you
for years and years
every fucking night
when you already had melatonin
but that silly little bird
upstairs just doesn't want to stop.
Sadness that grips you
like an abusive boyfriend
at a family lunch,
when your mom
asks about how you've been.
That's the shit that leads to suicide.

Some people will always be sad,
just like murderers and sexy movie stars;
they were just born that way.
And so like some murderers
and if we're honest, most movie stars
they have quite addictive personalities.
But meth makes you so tired
(they're already always tired,
how is that even fun?)

And cocaine might just
give you enough energy
to kill yourself,
Its craving pain that shows you true sadness
Craving to feel something different
than what you feel every day.
At least if you get dumped
you can cry
about something other than
that loved one who died last spring.
And each time it has to hurt
more than the last time
otherwise it doesn't hurt at all.
No rehab for that kind of addiction,
Just pills from pricks with PhDs.

MIDDING

Rain patters leaves in the yard
They bounce with the drops
like children on trampolines.

There's a breeze
blowing in the smell of
water-darkened wood and rocks.
The smell of earth
and the smell of the musty
aluminum mesh of the window screen
that catches the raindrops
like dust in cobwebs.

Big band music
filtered through the carpet,
And the walls and doors
wanders into the room.
The trumpets and piano
Swinging in softly
muffled in a way only you know;
Only in the way that is muffled
by where the record player sits in the living room
by the way the textures
of your furniture absorb the sound.
Muffled in the only way it can by your home
It's Harry James and his orchestra.

But only for you and only in this moment.

Someone's baking something;
The house is always so full
of the smells of breads
and pies and casseroles.
They all just sort of blend
Into one very distinct perfume of baking;
Your mother and your siblings baking.

Your father's fire
of newspapers and old wood
glows in that old brick fireplace.
Everyone is warm
Everyone is safe
Safe in the next room over.

A MOMENT OF TANGENCY

There's a girl sitting on bench
waiting for her train.
She's been looking up at the clouds
seeing so many amazing things;
Just up there
in the clouds
Things that she wants
so desperately to tell
to someone willing to listen.
There's so many stories in the clouds
if you just looked,
if you just listened to the girl
with the stories of the clouds
waiting for her train.

On the train there is a boy
staring out the window,
wondering what people see in the clouds.
They're just clouds to him
they will always just be clouds;
What else could they be?
They are beautiful but
so is the ocean.
It doesn't mean it's not
just water in the end,
But some part of him knows

they can't just be clouds.
People have to stare at the sky for a reason;
He just needs someone to explain
what's truly up with the clouds.

The train arrives at the station,
The boy looks down
The girl looks down
He smiles down at her on the bench
She smiles up at him in the window
She gets in the car behind him
It looked less crowded.

WISHING WELL

I walk around the wishing well
with armfuls of pennies
tossing them in dozens at a time.
Wishing it would be easy
Wishing it would be over
Wishing they would come back
Wishing it was different
Wishing anything was different.

HAPPINESS

The castle's in the sand,
splendid in its decadence
strong in its foundation.

But the tide is rolling in
and you must save the castle
before it's far too late.
You scramble to grab pieces
but then that tide sets in,
Taking that sandcastle
in its cold, consuming arms.

The castle's all but gone now
Echoes in the sand.
All that's left is that last piece
falling through your hand.

SEVEN

When I was just a child
I had my special seven.
My special seven people
that I loved more than anyone.
But now that I am all grown up
none of them remain.
You see in fifth grade my dad left
and left me with just six,
and then just two years later
Howie passed away
peaceful while he slept;
He left me with five.
And then six more months later
my mom passed away,
full of sorrow with a gunshot
She left me with four.
And then two more years later
my sister ran away
and left me with three more.
I moved and moved again
and lost my closest friends.
The other two grew up
and found some other people
and now I'm grown
and I'm alone
wondering where they went.

Which ones I miss the most
Obsessing over conversations
like lawyers and liars
yelling in my head
All day.
Fighting over which one I would've picked to stay,
Which one of the seven
hurt the most by leaving?
God, I just wish one had stayed.

GLASS ISN'T GOOD FOR YOUR LUNGS

My love for you is shattered glass
scattered around my thoughts
like ashes in an ocean,
and here I am
grabbing at the shards
holding them tight,
while they cut my hands
beyond repair;
and I hold these fistfuls of glass
up to my face
not wanting it to be over.
And now the dust is
peeling away my throat
and the insides of my lungs.
I am hacking and retching
blood and tears thrown off my face,
and my hands filled with glass
and that's how I die,
Gripping glass and choking on it.

TOY

I'd give you my eyes
so that you could see yourself
the way I do.
I'd give you my heart
just so you could love yourself
as much as I love you.
I'd give you my skin
So you could feel the rain
for the first time again.
I'd give you my lungs
so you could take a breath
of fresh air in the sun.
I'd give you my ears
so you could hear your lovely voice,
music just as words.
I swear to you I'd die for you
as long as you would smile,
and I'd give you my whole heart
beating so so strong,
but you have it already
and you don't even care.

THE MONSTERS UNDER THE BED

I searched for them for years
staring in my closet,
picking apart shadows
from piles of clothes
and trinkets in the dark.
Every single night
I searched under my bed,
knowing for sure that while I sleep
and dream and wake up in cold sweats
that that is where they come from.
And I questioned all my friends
demanding to know who they really were,
demanding to know why they did what they had to do
but they were never there.
Not in my friends or in my closet
or underneath my bed,
All these terrifying monsters
are all inside my head.

MAKING OUT

I was kissed by earth today
and as she pulled me in
the world around me darkened.
Greys like the greys of mountain rocks
when the sun sets just behind them.
Blues like the blues in ocean
the Atlantic, at the edge of the sunlight's rays
where the light fades into that cast abyss.
Purples like lilacs at twilight
softly held me while the others prayed.
It was some great storm
Heavy air enveloping.
I might as well have been sitting
at the bottom of a pool
in the dark
in the rain.
The world slows down just slightly
and then between my eyes
a kiss from heavenly skies.
A chill runs down my spine
and then we bring back time,
Falling all around me
angelic gifts from earth
Raindrops kissing skin.

ORANGE

They say the fruits with scars
are always the sweetest;
He was one scarred fruit for sure
An orange
covered in slashes.

With that thick peel
that feels akin to textured walls
that make houses look more like home.

But beyond the sweet he was full
of citrus
zest and charm and character.
My favorite fruit
My sweet scarred simple orange.

SILVER SWEETHEARTS

Lovers love lying.
Silver tongues sell sweet sounds.
Naive cynics that die trying,
to wear their hearts as crowns.

These cynics can't know better,
for they know no single difference,
between love that deserves letters,
and short-lived youthful ignorance.

But true lovers know,
They've seen it all before.
And still, they force sick love to grow,
These sour silver sweethearts lying till their lips are sore.

Plastic dolls are plastic dolls
We cannot play forever.

JIGSAW MEMORY

The third plank from the doorway
has a crack running down the side of it.
The laminate cover is peeling
on the edges,
I don't think you've noticed yet.
There's a chip in the paint
on the wall above your dresser,
It's in between your self portraits
and that picture your mom drew.
It sits right above the dead
flowers and books that line your dresser.
The way the light
hits it from this angle on your bed
makes the white contrast strangely
with the cream of the wall.
Your bed is crooked but your nightstands not;
Half the things in here aren't straight
but only barely so.
The bush outside your window's gotten bigger
Someday I'll regret this
not looking at your face
but you're not mine to look at;
And so I stare at the wall
and your floor,
down your hallway and out
your window.

I stare at everything but you;
And someday
When you're inevitably gone,
I'll piece you back together;
A little puzzle in my head.
I'll put together the edges
of your face and figure in the corners of my eyes;
The reflections of you in the mirror I saw
And that's how you'll exist;
Edges of memories in my mind
Bits and pieces of a face.
And someday the edges of those edges
will blur and fade away
like milk into coffee.
And someday all I'll have of you
will be images of walls and floors and doorways,
Blank and shining and silent.

CUPID IS YELLOW

Yellow the insult
Yellow as in coward
Yellow as in someone who can't finish the job.
He'll regret piercing my heart
with that arrowed tipped with gold.
He'll regret not having
the courage to kill me,
To use his talents with
Some arrow dipped in iron;
Not having the courage to finish the job
and pierce her heart as well.
I hope he feels this fucking shame, too
This shame that chips away at me inside,
as if I were a mountain to be mined.
I hope he's awake as long as I am
thinking of what he did wrong.
I hope he hates himself for this mistake;
I hope he sits up
Tearing out the feathers of wings;
Crying and screaming
As he rips his wings apart;
White feathers clutched by bloody hands.

FINAL THOUGHTS MEAN MORE
THAN FINAL WORDS

Imagine having the power
of being the last
thought someone has.
It matters not how often
you crossed their mind before,
You are eternally
the cherry on their life;
The last glowing ember
in a pile of ash.
Would I be the last thought
to dance around your mind?
Would I be anyone's?
Frozen for eternity
as the thing they deemed
more important than anything else;
That they wanted one last chance to see,
the thought that brought them comfort
when they needed it most.
I pine to be the final sentence,
The very last goodnight,
The last dance of neurons
fading to echoes of a favorite song.
You will populate my dreams in death;
You will walk through the decrepit
halls of my forgotten mind.

And even in death, I will smile
and though you might not hear me,
I'd like to thank you for coming.

IS CYANIDE SWEET ?

As a cynic I can't help
but make life sour.
And so I sit in hatred
of people that I'll never know;
Sweet people bitter
like stale vinegar;
Sweet people with their sugar souls;
Chewed up and spit out
by my misanthropic mind
That doesn't trust
the sugar to be sweet.
But to trust the sugar,
to trust the sweet,
That's to love.
Loving them means losing them
to time or distance or bitter true betrayal.
These days I cannot trust the sun to rise
so how can I be sure…
that sugar isn't cyanide.

SCRATCH PAPER

Write your sorrows in my skin,
Etch them with your knives and nails.
Write your pain across my heart until it bleeds, the beating
and the breathing stop.
Use me as your canvas
to paint some picture of your life.
Use me to give it meaning,
To show some hidden truth.
Then in the end
throw me to the wind and rain.
Burn me in your citrus candles
Toss me out like scratch paper
I've fulfilled my purpose.
Now day by day I rot away,
Your words scarred in my skin.
I was only here for one thing anyway,
To take away your pains and scars;
To heal all the deepest cuts and bruises on your bones,
So some far better soul
Could fill your heart with love
to pump around your brand-new body.
To give you life to write sweet letters
that you don't throw away.

IF GODS A PHOTOGRAPHER

Life's a blown-out photograph
far too overexposed.
You can almost see the edges of an image
Something beautiful that's worth a frame of film,
but blinding whiteness drowns it out;
Taken by some misguided portrait artist
with a keen eye for beauty
and a serious lack of technical ability.

HONEY STICKS

Howard bought me honey sticks
at farmer's markets and garden shops,
The memories of which
are far sweeter and more succulent
than the honey itself.
You and thoughts of you come to this broken bitter mind
of mine
bringing with sweet honey.
Hints of honey in Burt's Bees Chapstick when we kiss;
And though so many call it fire in your hair,
I see the sunshine in sweet, strawberry, honey sticks
when wishful winds blow wisps of your hair in with mine.
The honey Howard bought me was undoubtedly sweet
yet not so sweet as its strong memory.
But sweeter still is you, my love;
The honey in your whispers, lips and hair
The honey in your heart
that gushes into me
filling me with sweet sugar and smiles,
just like the honey sticks
that Howard used to buy.

ODE TO STRANGER

I want to thank the stranger
standing across the way.
The glowing, once young
stranger, that asked about my day.

I took comfort
in just seeing your sweater.
Cream, cable knit
tucked gently
into oversized, brown, dress pants.
Blowing like nautical flags
or silk scarves in the wind.
The cool wind
Carrying the rain on its back.

I took comfort
in your smile from across the street.
A smile bright
like oranges and lemons
in the morning sunshine.
A smile kind
like smiles worn by mothers
when they point up to the stars
and say, "Look honey,
Look how bright they shine tonight."

I took comfort in your voice.
A mellow voice,
like chamomile tea
that's finally cool enough to drink.
A voice soft like sunshine,
falling through a canopy of leaves;
The only voice that asked
if I was okay.
O, stranger, sweet stranger
who lives without context
without malice, or mind.
Offering your ears
like scratch paper
for me to scribble into
before we walked away.

One can always trust
a stranger, with the secrets of the day
Who better than a stranger?
A blank figure on the street.
Who better than someone,
who's no one to anyone?
Who's something to you
and only you today.
Who better than a stranger
that asks about your day.

TRAMPLE

The city is trampled
into this train.
You can see it in the scuffs
along the seats,
the chips in safety
paint running along the platform,
the concrete dust and asphalt
filling up the wedges
in floors designed for extra traction.

You can hear it in the rattling
Of paint cans echoing down the tunnels
like the skittering of rats
claws on concrete,
in the hum of glowing fluorescent lights
The kind that buzz on a zoom recorder.

Dead men stand apart
with sunken hollow
faces staring out windows and at walls
riding into the city of damned souls.

They stand though there are places they can sit,
pretending to be human;
Not wanting to be animals
fighting over scraps of meat.

Still, they stand and stand apart
not looking at the faces
of other corpses riding on the train.
Men in three-piece blended polyester suits
cannot associate
with those in leather jackets and bell-bottoms.

They look an awful lot like shellshock
Victims from the war to end all wars.
Not the first one or the second one
but the classist, capitalist war on the poor.

But on this train, they are all trampled together
and they can stiffen;
Like statues made of dust and steel
They can hold on to rails
till their knuckles turn white.
And their fingers look like fat, white spiders
gripping to cold steel.
And they can shuffle apart
like there's some bastard with a whip
commanding them never to touch.
Maybe there is.

In the next 5-15 minutes
Some vacant
empty
voice announces that this line has ended,

and so, they stumble off and stumble on.

The train will be more crowded
when they return tonight;
even standing they will be smashed
shoulder to shoulder
like bones in overcrowded graveyards.

Maybe they'll grow used to it;
Feel some connection
in the brushing
of leather and polyester.

Maybe when they stand together
and stand a little straighter;
Brave soldiers on a sinking ship.

The city and its people
are trampled into the train.
Bits and pieces of people
some soul, some skin
pounded
stomped
into the train.
Someday they will collect it all
the souls and skin and tears.
They will be together in the pain
And they will give it up together then.
All they are or would be

to some dark
and balding man
straightening his tie
and handing them a pen.

A SEED

I woke that April morning with dread inside my heart. My room was dark, as always, the blinds pulled tightly shut. The sunshine fell through slits along the edges, showing all that dust. I looked down at my shaking hands and balled them tight into fists. I could feel that dull pain creeping up my forearms as I tried to make it stop. But all that I accomplished was hyperventilation. So I pulled my pillow close and shut my eyes real tight. Maybe if I could not see, I'd forget that I was on the verge of tears. But still now, with my slowed-down breathing and the darkness in my eyes, I could not get control of this mad and frantic dread.

You see, that April morning, I had woken from this dream. This dream where they all left me. All the ones I loved. Where my dad who worked too often never once came home. And my grandpa, who I loved so dearly, went to bed one random night and never woke again. But the part that always stuck with me was the end in which my mom died. She sunk into this dark and sullen lake, surrounded by this heavy fog. I remember seeing that last wisp of fog follow her lips down to the water, as she gasped one final breath.

I wanted to run from my own head. The pounding of my heart echoed around my skull as my shut eyes replayed the dream over and over in my head. So I opened them up slowly and let go of the pillow. The concern was no longer in my head but in the world around me. More so in the sound of lack thereof. You see, my house was old and often creaked quite loudly. So on that April morning, when I heard nothing at all, my dread settled deeper, because I thought that nightmare might not be a nightmare. That maybe while I slept the whole world got turned upside down. That everyone was gone, and I was all alone.

So I ran into the hallway, looking all around. I checked my brother's room, and he was safe and sound asleep. And so I checked my parents' room, and that's when I started to panic. No one resided in that oversized King bed, that always held at least one of my parents.

The sun was not yet fully up, even though its first few rays peaked across the windowsill. I could feel my breathing getting heavier again. The tears began to slowly fall, tickling my cheeks as they did. I ran downstairs frantically, to see if anyone was left. And I thought it was beyond all hope, but my mother sat at the kitchen table, sipping on her hot peppermint tea. She looked up from online paper to see me standing on the stairs, trying to recover from the most relieving shock that I have ever had in my entire life.

"Are you all right? You look upset, Cai," she said softly, with genuine concern.

I could not believe my eyes, let alone muster the words to speak. I rushed over and hugged her tightly where she sat.

"You're alive," I said quietly, my voice muffled by her shirt that was slightly damp from my tears.

Her hands felt like soft sunshine, warm from the heat of her morning coffee. And she stroked my hair so gently, almost like a breeze.

"Of course I'm alive," she said quietly, just loud enough for us to hear.

I finally slowed my breathing and collected my thoughts. I let out the deepest breath and, almost choking on my words, I said, "You're still here."

She let me go a little and fixed my messy hair. And with those sunshine hands of hers, she wiped away my tears. She said to me, seriously and with such unending care, "Of course I'm here. I'll always be here."

And choking on my words again, I said to her, "You promise?"

In this single moment, she held in her hands my life, my hope, my future. And knowing all that had been and was to come, she looked into my crying eyes and gave to me this tiny seed — this seed of hope and trust. This seed that said, "I promise". She planted it so simply, with my fearful tears for water and her sunshine hands for warmth. It grew for years and years on end. With all this tender love and care, this formed a luscious, pink rose — a rose without a thorn.

But then her sunlight died away, and as the years drew on, the colors lost their glow. The rose that grew had darkened, and it grew so many thorns; fueled by moonlight and the stars, those cold and distant lights. This rose of hope and trust and love, stays until it's bitter end, when all that's left is thorns, and the black and fallen petals strewn around the stem.